welcome TO TH[E]
PARTY!

THIS BOOK BELONGS TO: ....

PARTY DATE: ....

PEOPLE AT THE PARTY: ....

....

....

....

PARTY THEME: ....

TIME WE WENT TO BED: ....

FIRST PERSON TO FALL ASLEEP: ....

LAST PERSON AWAKE: ....

FOODS WE ATE: ....

FUNNIEST PARTY MOMENT: ....

MOMENT WE'RE MOST LIKELY TO REMEMBER:

....

sleepover NICKNAME

MATCH THE **FIRST LETTER OF YOUR NAME** WITH THE **MONTH YOU WERE BORN** TO FIND OUT YOUR SLUMBER PARTY NICKNAME! EVERYONE SHOULD CALL YOU THAT FOR THE REST OF THE SLEEPOVER!

A-JELLYBEAN	N-HAPPY	**JAN**: SNORES-A-LOT
B-BUBBLE	O-SLEEPY	**FEB**: FEET
C-SUGAR	P-FUZZY	**MARCH**: DREAMER
D-PEANUT	Q-APPLE	**APRIL**: ANGEL
E-PICKLE	R-HONEY	**MAY**: POP
F-DUCKIE	S-TEENY	**JUNE**: SNOOZER
G-BANANA	T-CHEEKY	**JULY**: NUGGET
H-BESTIE	U-DJ	**AUG**: NOODLE
I-COOKIE	V-TWINKLE	**SEPT**: TOOTS
J-TINY	W-KITTY	**OCT**: JAMMIES
K-FLUFFY	X-CANDY	**NOV**: CAT
L-JOLLY	Y-CUTIE	**DEC**: QUEEN
M-DANCING	Z-GIGGLE	

WRITE YOUR SLEEPOVER
PARTY NICKNAME HERE:

TABLE of CONTENTS

1. TRUTH OR DARE..........................PAGE 5

2. ALL ABOUT MY BESTIES.................PAGE 19

3. WOULD YOU RATHER.....................PAGE 31

4. JOKE'S ON YOU...........................PAGE 43

5. SLEEPOVER RECIPES......................PAGE 55

6. SLEEPOVER GAMES.......................PAGE 77

7. M.A.S.H...................................PAGE 89

Z
Z
Z

TRUTH or DARE!

5

TRUTH or DARE?

TAKE TURNS, AND CHOOSE IF YOU
WOULD RATHER DO THE TRUTH OR DARE.

TRUTH WHAT'S THE FUNNIEST THING THAT'S EVER HAPPENED TO YOU AT SCHOOL?

DARE PUT ON LIPSTICK WITHOUT A MIRROR HAVING THE PERSON TO YOUR RIGHT TELL YOU HOW.

TRUTH WHAT'S THE MOST ANNOYING SOUND TO YOU?

DARE DO A HANDSTAND.

TRUTH IF YOU WON A MILLION DOLLARS, WHAT'S THE FIRST THING YOU WOULD BUY?

DARE SING PART OF A TAYLOR SWIFT SONG.

TRUTH or DARE?

TAKE TURNS, AND CHOOSE IF YOU
WOULD RATHER DO THE TRUTH OR DARE.

TRUTH WHAT FOOD DO YOU HOPE YOU NEVER HAVE TO EAT AGAIN?

DARE WEAR A TOWEL OR BLANKET AS YOUR PERSONAL CAPE FOR THE REST OF THE GAME.

TRUTH HOW MANY TIMES A DAY DO YOU *REALLY* BRUSH YOUR TEETH?

DARE WASH YOUR HANDS USING BUTTER INSTEAD OF SOAP.

TRUTH WHAT'S YOUR FAVORITE RIDE AT AN AMUSEMENT PARK?

DARE DRAW A PICTURE USING YOUR TOES.

TRUTH or DARE?

*TAKE TURNS, AND CHOOSE IF YOU
WOULD RATHER DO THE TRUTH OR DARE.*

TRUTH — DO YOUR PARENTS HAVE A NICKNAME FOR YOU? WHAT IS IT?

DARE — DO JUMPING JACKS UNTIL YOUR NEXT TURN.

TRUTH — WHAT ARE YOU MOST AFRAID OF?

DARE — SNIFF YOUR FRIEND'S FEET.

TRUTH — IF YOU HAD THREE WISHES, WHAT WOULD THEY BE?

DARE — LET THE PERSON TO YOUR LEFT STYLE YOUR HAIR.

TRUTH or DARE?

TAKE TURNS, AND CHOOSE IF YOU
WOULD RATHER DO THE TRUTH OR DARE.

TRUTH WHEN WAS THE LAST TIME YOU CLEANED YOUR ROOM?

DARE BITE INTO A SLICE OF LEMON.

TRUTH WHAT'S YOUR WEIRDEST TALENT?

DARE PAT YOUR HEAD AND RUB YOUR TUMMY WHILE COUNTING TO 15.

TRUTH HAVE YOU EVER SNOOPED TO SEE YOUR CHRISTMAS OR BIRTHDAY PRESENTS?

DARE OPEN THE DOOR AND YELL OUT "MERRY CHRISTMAS TO ALL AND TO ALL A GOOD NIGHT!"

TRUTH or DARE?

TRUTH WHAT CARTOON CHARACTER ARE YOU MOST LIKE?

DARE DO YOUR BEST ROBOT DANCE FOR 30 SECONDS.

TRUTH IF YOU COULD CHANGE ONE THING ABOUT YOURSELF, WHAT WOULD IT BE?

DARE EAT A SPOONFUL OF SUGAR.

TRUTH IF YOU COULD ONLY SHOP AT ONE STORE FOR THE REST OF YOUR LIFE, WHERE WOULD IT BE?

DARE WIGGLE AROUND ON THE GROUND LIKE A SNAKE.

TRUTH or DARE?

TAKE TURNS, AND CHOOSE IF YOU
WOULD RATHER DO THE TRUTH OR DARE.

TRUTH WHAT'S THE CLUMSIEST THING YOU'VE EVER DONE?

DARE TRY TO LICK YOUR ELBOW WHILE MEOWING.

TRUTH WHAT'S THE GROSSEST FOOD YOUR PARENTS MAKE?

DARE EAT CEREAL AND MILK WITHOUT USING YOUR HANDS.

TRUTH IF YOU COULD CHANGE ONE THING ABOUT YOUR PAST, WHAT WOULD IT BE?

DARE SPIN IN A CIRCLE TEN TIMES, THEN TRY TO WALK IN A STRAIGHT LINE.

TRUTH or DARE?

TAKE TURNS, AND CHOOSE IF YOU
WOULD RATHER DO THE TRUTH OR DARE.

TRUTH WHAT IS YOUR FAVORITE MEMORY FROM THE LAST SCHOOL YEAR?

DARE END EVERY SENTENCE FOR THE REST OF THE GAME WITH, "AND THAT'S WHEN I LOST MY PANTS!"

TRUTH WHICH CELEBRITY WOULD YOU WANT TO BE, AND WHY?

DARE EVERY TIME THE PERSON TO YOUR RIGHT SPEAKS, PAT THEM ON THE HEAD AND SAY, "GOOD PUPPY."

TRUTH IF YOU OPENED A RESTAURANT WHAT TYPE OF FOOD WOULD YOU SERVE?

DARE WRITE YOUR NAME HOLDING THE PENCIL IN YOUR MOUTH.

TRUTH or DARE?

TAKE TURNS, AND CHOOSE IF YOU
WOULD RATHER DO THE TRUTH OR DARE.

TRUTH — WHAT'S THE WEIRDEST DREAM YOU'VE EVER HAD?

DARE — DANCE WITH NO MUSIC ON.

TRUTH — WHAT'S YOUR LEAST FAVORITE FOOD?

DARE — SING YOUR FAVORITE DISNEY PRINCESS SONG.

TRUTH — WHAT MOVIE TITLE BEST DESCRIBES YOUR LIFE?

DARE — HOLD AN ICE CUBE IN YOUR MOUTH FOR AS LONG AS YOU CAN.

TRUTH or DARE?

TRUTH — WHAT'S THE LAST LIE YOU TOLD?

DARE — AFTER EACH PLAYER'S TURN SAY, "AND THAT'S SHOW BUSINESS FOR YA!" FOR ONE ROUND.

TRUTH — WHAT PIECE OF CLOTHING DO YOU WEAR THE MOST?

DARE — PLAY THE AIR GUITAR TO A SONG OF CHOICE.

TRUTH — GIVE A COMPLIMENT TO THE PERSON ON YOUR LEFT.

DARE — GIVE A PIGGYBACK RIDE TO THE PERSON ON YOUR LEFT.

TRUTH or DARE?

TAKE TURNS, AND CHOOSE IF YOU
WOULD RATHER DO THE TRUTH OR DARE.

TRUTH WHAT CARTOON CHARACTER DOES THE PLAYER TO YOUR RIGHT LOOK LIKE?

DARE DO TEN PUSHUPS.

TRUTH HOW OFTEN DO YOU CLEAN YOUR ROOM?

DARE WEAR YOUR SHOES ON YOUR HEAD UNTIL YOUR NEXT TURN.

TRUTH WHAT'S THE FUNNIEST JOKE YOU KNOW?

DARE DO JAZZ HANDS EVERY TIME YOU SPEAK.

TRUTH or DARE?

TAKE TURNS, AND CHOOSE IF YOU
WOULD RATHER DO THE TRUTH OR DARE.

TRUTH — HAVE YOU EVER SNOOPED THROUGH YOUR PARENTS' MESSAGES?

DARE — JUMP ON ONE FOOT WHILE SINGING THE ABC'S.

TRUTH — WHAT'S YOUR FAVORITE SONG TO SING IN THE CAR?

DARE — BALANCE A SPOON ON YOUR NOSE AND COUNT TO TEN.

TRUTH — IF YOU COULD CHANGE ONE THING ABOUT YOUR FAMILY WHAT WOULD IT BE?

DARE — GO OUTSIDE AND YELL, "THE BRITISH ARE COMING; THE BRITISH ARE COMING!!"

TRUTH or DARE?

TAKE TURNS, AND CHOOSE IF YOU
WOULD RATHER DO THE TRUTH OR DARE.

TRUTH WHAT IS YOUR FAVORITE THING ABOUT THE PERSON ON YOUR RIGHT?

DARE SAY, "I'M A SILLY GOOSE!" WITH YOUR TONGUE STICKING OUT.

TRUTH WHAT'S YOUR FAVORITE VIDEO GAME?

DARE DO A TIKTOK DANCE.

TRUTH WOULD YOU RATHER HAVE THE POWER TO FLY OR TO BE INVISIBLE?

DARE DO A CARTWHEEL.

ALL about my BESTIES!

19

all about my BESTIES!

PICK THE PERSON AT YOUR SLUMBER PARTY WHO BEST FITS THE FOLLOWING DESCRIPTIONS. YOU CAN EVEN CHOOSE YOURSELF!

WHO'S MOST LIKELY TO BE ON A REALITY TV SHOW?

WHO WOULD KISS A FROG TO SEE IF IT TURNED INTO A PRINCE?

WHO TAKES THE LONGEST TO MAKE DECISIONS?

WHO IS MOST LIKELY TO EAT A BUG FOR $20?

all about my BESTIES!

PICK THE PERSON AT YOUR SLUMBER PARTY WHO BEST FITS THE FOLLOWING DESCRIPTIONS. YOU CAN EVEN CHOOSE YOURSELF!

WHO'S THE BEST AT KEEPING SECRETS?

WHO WOULD WEAR PAJAMAS ALL DAY IF THEY COULD?

WHO IS MOST LIKELY TO MARRY SOMEONE FROM SCHOOL?

WHO IS MOST LIKELY TO KNOW ALL THE SCHOOL GOSSIP?

all about my BESTIES!

PICK THE PERSON AT YOUR SLUMBER PARTY WHO BEST FITS THE FOLLOWING DESCRIPTIONS. YOU CAN EVEN CHOOSE YOURSELF!

WHO WILL BE ON THEIR PHONE/TABLET THE MOST TONIGHT?

WHO WILL BE THE FIRST TO TEXT THEIR MOM OR DAD, "GOOD NIGHT?"

WHO'S MOST LIKELY TO NOT ADMIT THEY LIKE THEIR CRUSH?

WHO IS MOST LIKELY TO BE FAMOUS ONE DAY?

all about my BESTIES!

PICK THE PERSON AT YOUR SLUMBER PARTY WHO BEST FITS THE FOLLOWING DESCRIPTIONS. YOU CAN EVEN CHOOSE YOURSELF!

WHO'S MOST LIKELY TO GET UP EARLY TO EXERCISE?

WHO ALWAYS HAS A SONG STUCK IN THEIR HEAD THAT THEY'RE HUMMING OR MUMBLING?

WHO BROUGHT THE MOST ORGANIZED OVERNIGHT BAG?

WHO'S MOST LIKELY TO SLEEPWALK TONIGHT?

all about my BESTIES!

PICK THE PERSON AT YOUR SLUMBER PARTY WHO BEST FITS THE FOLLOWING DESCRIPTIONS. YOU CAN EVEN CHOOSE YOURSELF!

WHO'S MOST LIKELY TO BE AN OLYMPIC ATHLETE?

WHO'S MOST LIKELY TO TALK ALL NIGHT ABOUT THEIR CRUSH?

WHO GIVES GREAT ADVICE WHEN SOMEONE IS SAD?

WHO IS MOST LIKELY TO TALK IN THEIR SLEEP?

all about my BESTIES!

PICK THE PERSON AT YOUR SLUMBER PARTY WHO BEST FITS THE FOLLOWING DESCRIPTIONS. YOU CAN EVEN CHOOSE YOURSELF!

WHO'S MOST LIKELY TO WAKE EVERYONE UP WITH THEIR SNORING?

WHO'S MOST LIKELY TO BE WEARING MISMATCHED SOCKS?

WHO'S MOST LIKELY TO PRANK SOMEONE TONIGHT?

WHO LAUGHS THE LOUDEST AT THEIR OWN JOKES?

all about my BESTIES!

PICK THE PERSON AT YOUR SLUMBER PARTY WHO BEST FITS THE FOLLOWING DESCRIPTIONS. YOU CAN EVEN CHOOSE YOURSELF!

WHO'S MOST LIKELY TO TRAVEL THE WORLD AFTER HIGH SCHOOL?

WHO'S MOST LIKELY TO TRIP AND FALL TONIGHT?

WHO'S MOST LIKELY TO TAKE SELFIES AT THE PARTY?

WHO COULD YOU SEE LIVING ON A FARM ONE DAY?

all about my BESTIES!

PICK THE PERSON AT YOUR SLUMBER PARTY WHO BEST FITS THE FOLLOWING DESCRIPTIONS. YOU CAN EVEN CHOOSE YOURSELF!

WHO'S MOST LIKELY TO FALL ASLEEP IF YOU PUT A MOVIE ON?

WHO'S MOST LIKELY TO BE LATE TO EVERY PARTY?

WHO'S MOST LIKELY TO MESSAGE A CRUSH FROM THE PARTY?

WHO'S MOST LIKELY TO SHARE THEIR STUFF?

all about my BESTIES!

PICK THE PERSON AT YOUR SLUMBER PARTY WHO BEST FITS THE FOLLOWING DESCRIPTIONS. YOU CAN EVEN CHOOSE YOURSELF!

WHO'S MOST LIKELY TO BE FILTHY RICH WHEN THEY'RE OLDER?

WHO AT THE PARTY HAS THE BEST SINGING VOICE?

WHO MAKES THE FUNNIEST FACES?

WHO WILL MISS THEIR PET THE MOST TONIGHT?

all about my

BESTIES!

PICK THE PERSON AT YOUR SLUMBER PARTY WHO BEST FITS THE FOLLOWING DESCRIPTIONS. YOU CAN EVEN CHOOSE YOURSELF!

WHO WILL BE THE FIRST TO GET MARRIED?

WHO'S MOST LIKELY TO SLEEP THROUGH AN ALARM?

WHO'S MOST LIKELY TO RUN FOR PRESIDENT ONE DAY?

WHO'S MOST LIKELY TO LOSE SOMETHING AT THE PARTY TONIGHT?

would you rather?

Would you Rather?

WHICH PET WOULD YOU RATHER HAVE?

◯ A PET DRAGON   ◯ A PET UNICORN

WHICH VACATION WOULD YOU RATHER GO ON?

◯ AN ADVENTUROUS VACATION   ◯ A RELAXING VACATION

WOULD YOU RATHER ONLY EAT:

◯ COLD FOOD   ◯ HOT FOOD

WOULD YOU RATHER BE:

◯ 30 MINUTES EARLY FOR   ◯ 5 MINUTES LATE
EVERYTHING   FOR EVERYTHING

Would you Rather?

WOULD YOU RATHER HAVE TO:

◯ CRAWL EVERYWHERE   ◯ SKIP EVERYWHERE

WHERE WOULD YOU RATHER LIVE?

◯ A SMALL FARM TOWN   ◯ A BIG CITY

WOULD YOU RATHER:

◯ BE AN ONLY CHILD   ◯ HAVE 10 SIBLINGS

WHICH WOULD YOU RATHER DO WHILE SLEEPING?

◯ SNORE LOUDLY ENOUGH TO WAKE EVERYONE UP   ◯ SLEEPWALK THROUGH THE HOUSE

Would you Rather?

WOULD YOU RATHER LIVE:

◯ 100 YEARS IN THE PAST   ◯ 100 YEARS IN THE FUTURE

WOULD YOU RATHER GO A DAY WITHOUT:

◯ TALKING TO PEOPLE   ◯ YOUR TABLET

WHICH WOULD YOU RATHER WIN?

◯ NINJA WARRIOR   ◯ THE VOICE

WHICH HAIRSTYLE WOULD YOU RATHER HAVE?

◯ RAINBOW-STRIPED HAIR   ◯ CHEETAH PRINT HAIR

Would you Rather?

WOULD YOU RATHER HAVE:

◯ THE SAME SONG STUCK IN YOUR HEAD FOR A MONTH

◯ THE SAME DREAM EVERY NIGHT FOR A YEAR

WOULD YOU RATHER OWN:

◯ YOUR OWN BOAT

◯ YOUR OWN PLANE

WHICH WOULD YOU RATHER WEAR ALL DAY LONG?

◯ A SCHOOL UNIFORM

◯ PAJAMAS

WOULD YOU RATHER BE:

◯ SUPER TALL

◯ SUPER SHORT

Would you Rather?

WHICH SUPER POWER WOULD YOU RATHER HAVE?

◯ THE ABILITY TO READ MINDS   ◯ THE ABILITY TO FLY

WOULD YOU RATHER HAVE TO:

◯ SING EVERY TIME YOU TALK   ◯ DANCE EVERY TIME YOU WALK

WOULD YOU RATHER SLEEP WITHOUT:

◯ A BLANKET   ◯ A PILLOW

WOULD YOU RATHER SPEND THE NIGHT AT:

◯ AN AMUSEMENT PARK   ◯ THE ZOO

Would you Rather?

WOULD YOU RATHER EAT DINNER:

◯ WITH YOUR FAMILY AT THE DINNER TABLE

◯ ALONE IN YOUR ROOM

WOULD YOU RATHER:

◯ TELL SOMEONE YOU'RE ANGRY

◯ KEEP YOUR FEELINGS TO YOURSELF

WOULD YOU RATHER HAVE:

◯ UNLIMITED DONUTS

◯ UNLIMITED CHIPS

WOULD YOU RATHER PLAY :

◯ SOCCER WEARING HIGH HEELS

◯ BASKETBALL WEARING ROLLER SKATES

Would you Rather?

WOULD YOU RATHER HAVE:

◯ A TON OF ACQUAINTANCES   ◯ ONLY 2 CLOSE FRIENDS

WHICH WOULD YOU RATHER HAVE FOR LUNCH?

◯ A FRESH AND HEALTHY SALAD   ◯ A JUICY CHEESEBURGER

WOULD YOU RATHER:

◯ HAVE A FRIEND MESSAGE YOU   ◯ HAVE A FRIEND VIDEO CALL YOU

WOULD YOU RATHER BE ABLE TO:

◯ SLIDE DOWN RAINBOWS   ◯ BOUNCE ON CLOUDS

Would you Rather?

WOULD YOU RATHER WIN:

◯ AN OLYMPIC GOLD MEDAL   ◯ AN ACADEMY AWARD

WOULD YOU RATHER:

◯ GET GOOD GRADES   ◯ BE GOOD AT SPORTS

WOULD YOU RATHER BE:

◯ THE AGE YOU CURRENTLY ARE   ◯ JUMP AHEAD 5 YEARS INTO THE FUTURE

WHICH JOB WOULD YOU RATHER HAVE IN A MOVIE:

◯ STUNT PERSON   ◯ ACTOR / ACTRESS

Would you Rather?

WOULD YOU RATHER BE ABLE TO:

◯ SWIM LIKE A DOLPHIN   ◯ FLY LIKE A BIRD

WOULD YOU RATHER LIVE THE REST OF YOUR LIFE:

◯ AS A MERMAID   ◯ AS A TINY FAIRY

WOULD YOU RATHER HAVE:

◯ CAKE FROSTING FOR HAIR   ◯ BIRTHDAY CANDLES FOR TEETH

WOULD YOU RATHER:

◯ HAVE YOUR PARENTS CHOOSE WHO YOU MARRY   ◯ BE SINGLE FOREVER

Would you Rather?

WOULD YOU RATHER HAVE:

◯ AN EXTRA ARM   ◯ AN EXTRA LEG

WOULD YOU RATHER:

◯ FIND $100 AND KEEP IT   ◯ FIND $500 AND GIVE IT AWAY TO CHARITY

WOULD YOU RATHER:

◯ PLAY THE HERO IN A MOVIE   ◯ PLAY THE VILLAIN IN A MOVIE

WOULD YOU RATHER:

◯ VACATION IN A TREE HOUSE   ◯ VACATION IN AN IGLOO

JOKE'S on YOU!

JOKE'S on you!

QUESTION: WHY DID THE COOKIE GO TO THE DOCTOR?

ANSWER: *HE FELT CRUMBY!*

QUESTION: WHAT DO YOU GET WHEN YOU CROSS
AN ELEPHANT AND A FISH?

ANSWER: *SWIMMING TRUNKS!*

QUESTION: WHY CAN'T YOUR HAND BE 12 INCHES
LONG?

ANSWER: *BECAUSE IT WOULD BE A FOOT!*

JOKE'S on you!

QUESTION: WHAT DOES A SPY DO IN BED?

ANSWER: *GOES UNDERCOVER!*

QUESTION: WHY SHOULDN'T YOU TELL A SECRET
IN A CORN FIELD?

ANSWER: *THERE ARE TOO MANY EARS!*

QUESTION: HOW DO YOU PLAN AN OUTER SPACE
PARTY?

ANSWER: *YOU PLANET!*

JOKE'S on you!

QUESTION: HOW DOES A SKELETON START A LETTER?

ANSWER: *TOMB WHOM IT MAY CONCERN!*

QUESTION: WHY DID THE GOLFER WEAR TWO PAIRS OF PANTS?

ANSWER: *IN CASE HE GOT A HOLE IN ONE!*

QUESTION: HOW DO YOU STOP A BULL FROM CHARGING?

ANSWER: *CANCEL ITS CREDIT CARDS!*

JOKE'S on you!

QUESTION: WHY DO BEES HAVE STICKY HAIR?

ANSWER: *BECAUSE THEY USE A HONEYCOMB!*

QUESTION: WHAT DID MAMA CORN SAY TO
BABY CORN?

ANSWER: *"WHERE'S POP-CORN?"*

QUESTION: WHY DID THE POT SAY GOODBYE TO THE
BOILING WATER?

ANSWER: *BECAUSE IT WILL BE MIST!*

JOKE'S on you!

QUESTION: WHAT DO YOU CALL A FAKE NOODLE?

ANSWER: *AN IMPASTA!*

QUESTION: WHAT BREED OF DOG CAN JUMP HIGHER
THAN A BUILDING?

ANSWER: *ALL OF THEM - BUILDINGS CAN'T JUMP!*

QUESTION: WHAT KIND OF BIRTHDAY DO YOU
THROW FOR A JANITOR?

ANSWER: *A SUPPLIES PARTY!*

JOKE'S on you!

QUESTION: WHY ARE THERE NO JOKES ABOUT PIZZA?

ANSWER: *THEY'RE ALL TOO CHEESY!*

QUESTION: WHY DO ASTRONAUTS STAY AWAY
FROM CROWDS?

ANSWER: *BECAUSE THEY LIKE SPACE!*

QUESTION: WHAT DO YOU CALL A FISH WITH
FOUR EYES?

ANSWER: *FIIIISH!*

JOKE'S on you!

QUESTION: WHAT TIME DOES A DUCK WAKE UP?

ANSWER: *AT THE QUACK OF DAWN!*

QUESTION: WHAT DID ONE PLATE WHISPER TO THE OTHER PLATE?

ANSWER: *DINNER'S ON ME TONIGHT!*

QUESTION: WHAT DID ONE TOILET SAY TO THE OTHER?

ANSWER: *YOU LOOK A BIT FLUSHED!*

JOKE'S on you!

QUESTION: WHY ARE MOUNTAINS SO FUNNY?

ANSWER: *THEY'RE HILL AREAS!*

QUESTION: WHY ARE CATS ALWAYS SO GOOD AT VIDEO GAMES?

ANSWER: *BECAUSE THEY HAVE NINE LIVES!*

QUESTION: WHAT'S RED AND SMELLS LIKE BLUE PAINT?

ANSWER: *RED PAINT!*

JOKE'S on you!

QUESTION: HOW DO CELEBRITIES STAY SO COOL?

ANSWER: *THEY HAVE A LOT OF FANS!*

QUESTION: WHAT DO YOU CALL A PENCIL WITH TWO ERASERS?

ANSWER: *POINTLESS!*

QUESTION: WHY IS IT HARD TO ANNOY A SKELETON?

ANSWER: *BECAUSE YOU CAN'T GET UNDER THEIR SKIN!*

JOKE'S on you!

QUESTION: WHY WAS THE BROOM LATE?

ANSWER: *IT OVER SWEPT!*

QUESTION: WHAT DID ONE ELEVATOR SAY TO THE OTHER ELEVATOR?

ANSWER: *I THINK I'M COMING DOWN WITH SOMETHING!*

QUESTION: WHY IS THE MATH BOOK ALWAYS SAD?

ANSWER: *IT HAS SO MANY PROBLEMS!*

sleepover RECIPES

MARSHMALLOW FRUIT DIP

MARSHMALLOW FRUIT DIP

THIS ONE IS SO SIMPLE BUT SOOO GOOD!!

TIP

PAIRS WELL WITH ANY FRUIT BUT OUR FAVORITE IS BANANAS!

INGREDIENTS

- 1 PACKAGE (8 OUNCES) CREAM CHEESE, SOFTENED
- 1 JAR (7 OUNCES) MARSHMALLOW CREME
- ASSORTED FRESH FRUIT

DIRECTIONS

IN A LARGE BOWL, BEAT CREAM CHEESE UNTIL BLENDED. FOLD IN MARSHMALLOW CREME. SERVE WITH FRUIT. ENJOY!

RAINBOW FRUIT & YOGURT PARFAITS

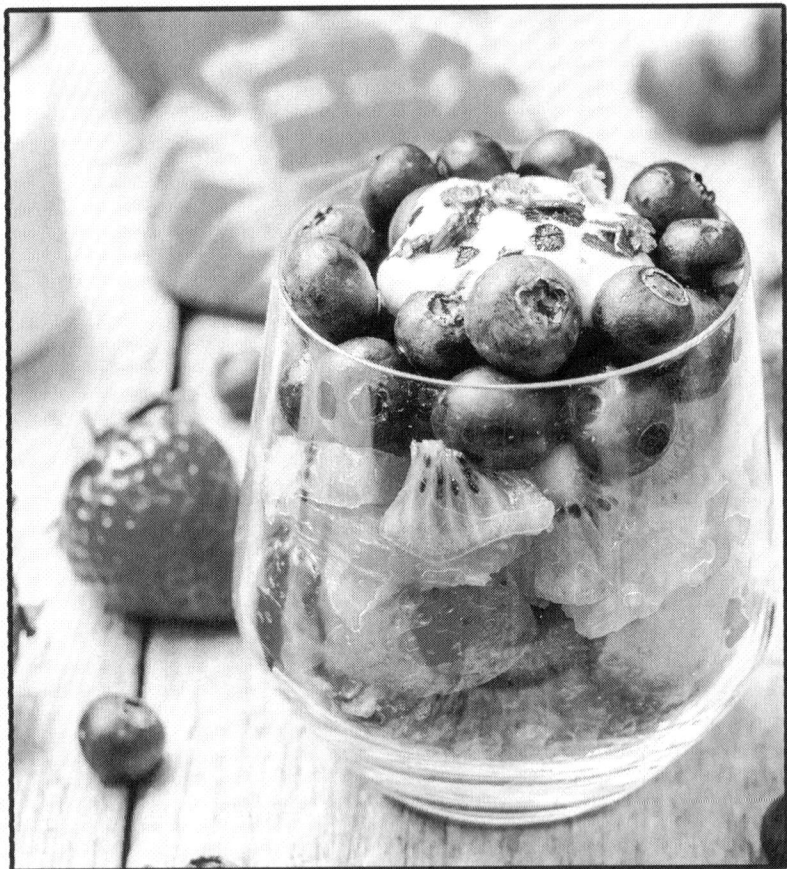

RAINBOW FRUIT & YOGURT PARFAITS

FRUIT PARFAITS MAKE WONDERFUL, COLORFUL, HEALTHY PARTY TREATS. TO MAKE IT FUN FOR A PARTY OR SLEEPOVER, SET OUT GLASSES AND LET EVERYONE BUILD THEIR OWN PARFAITS.

TIP: A BIT OF CEREAL OR GRANOLA ON TOP OF YOUR FRUIT AND YOGURT PARFAIT ADDS A FUN CRUNCH!

INGREDIENTS

- STRAWBERRIES
- CANTALOUPE CHUNKS
- ORANGE SLICES
- PINEAPPLE CHUNKS
- STAR FRUIT
- GREEN GRAPES
- KIWI
- BLUEBERRIES
- PURPLE GRAPES
- VANILLA YOGURT
- MINI MARSHMALLOWS, OPTIONAL
- CEREAL OR GRANOLA, OPTIONAL

DIRECTIONS

LAYER YOUR INGREDIENTS IN A GLASS. START WITH YOUR RED FRUIT AT THE BOTTOM, THEN A SMALL SCOOP OF VANILLA YOGURT, NEXT ADD ORANGE FRUIT, YOGURT, YELLOW FRUIT, YOGURT, GREEN FRUIT, YOGURT, BLUE FRUIT, YOGURT, AND TOP WITH PURPLE FRUIT. TOP WITH MINI MARSHMALLOWS, CEREAL OR GRANOLA, IF DESIRED.

Recipes

PINWHEEL ROLLUPS

PINWHEEL ROLLUPS

PINWHEEL ROLLUPS ARE A FUN AND EASY APPETIZER! SLUMBER PARTY GUESTS CAN "MAKE THEM THEIR OWN" BY CHOOSING THEIR MEAT AND CHEESES.

INGREDIENTS

- 3 LARGE TORTILLAS, LOOK FOR "BURRITO SIZE"
- 12 SLICES OF DELI MEAT - TURKEY AND HAM ARE GREAT OPTIONS
- 12 SLICES OF CHEESE - AMERICAN, CHEDDAR, OR PROVOLONE
- 6 TBSP CREAM CHEESE
- ROMAINE LETTUCE

DIRECTIONS

1. LAY THE TORTILLAS FLAT AND SPREAD ABOUT 2 TABLESPOONS OF CREAM CHEESE ON EACH.

2. LAYER 4 SLICES OF DELI MEAT ONTO THE TORTILLAS.

3. TOP THE MEAT WITH THE ROMAINE LETTUCE AND FOUR SLICES OF CHEESE.

4. ROLL THE TORTILLAS TIGHTLY, AND SLICE INTO 2-INCH SECTIONS. USE A TOOTHPICK OR REUSABLE FOOD PICKS TO SECURE EACH WHEEL.

POPCORN PARTY BAR

POPCORN PARTY BAR

POPCORN IS A SLEEPOVER NECESSITY, BUT YOU CAN PUT A TWIST ON TRADITIONAL BUTTERED POPCORN WITH A POPCORN BAR!

INGREDIENTS

- AIR-POPPED OR PLAIN MICROWAVABLE POPCORN
- CINNAMON SUGAR
- SEA SALT
- CHILI PEPPER (FOR THOSE WHO LIKE A LITTLE SPICE!)
- PARMESAN CHEESE
- MELTED BUTTER
- PEANUTS
- M&MS
- GUMMY CANDIES
- WHATEVER SOUNDS YUMMY!
- CUTE BAGS OR FUN CUPS

DIRECTIONS

GIVE EACH MEMBER OF THE PARTY A CUTE BAG OR CUP. SET A TABLE WITH BIG BOWLS OF POPCORN AND ALL THE DESIRED ACCOUTREMENTS. LET THE PARTY GOERS MIX THEIR OWN POPCORN SNACK CREATIONS.

Recipes

NO-BAKE SUNFLOWER BUTTER TREATS

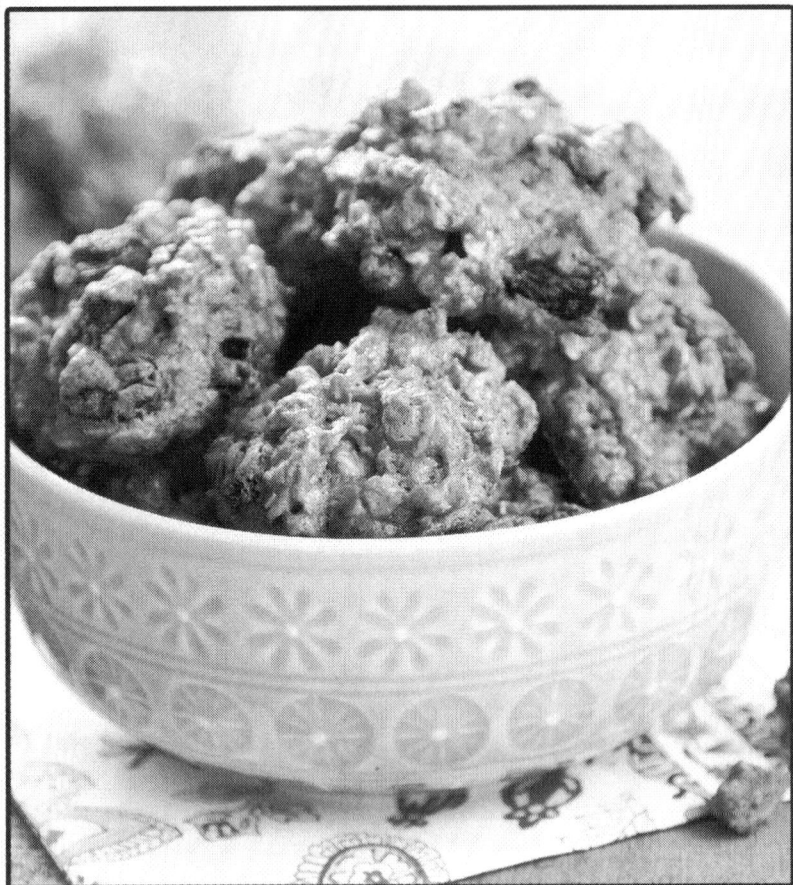

NO-BAKE SUNFLOWER BUTTER TREATS

SUNFLOWER BUTTER IS A GREAT ALTERNATIVE FOR ANY KIDS WITH A NUT ALLERGY. PLUS IT TASTES GREAT!

INGREDIENTS

- 1/3 CUP SUNFLOWER BUTTER
- 1/4 CUP HONEY
- 1/2 TEASPOON VANILLA EXTRACT
- 1/3 CUP NONFAT DRY MILK POWDER
- 1/3 CUP QUICK-COOKING OATS
- 2 TABLESPOONS GRAHAM CRACKER CRUMBS
- RAISINS (OPTIONAL)

DIRECTIONS

IN A SMALL BOWL, COMBINE THE SUNFLOWER BUTTER, HONEY AND VANILLA. STIR IN THE MILK POWDER, OATS AND GRAHAM CRACKER CRUMBS AND OPTIONAL RAISINS. SHAPE INTO ONE INCH BALLS. COVER AND REFRIGERATE UNTIL SERVING.

BANANA SUSHI

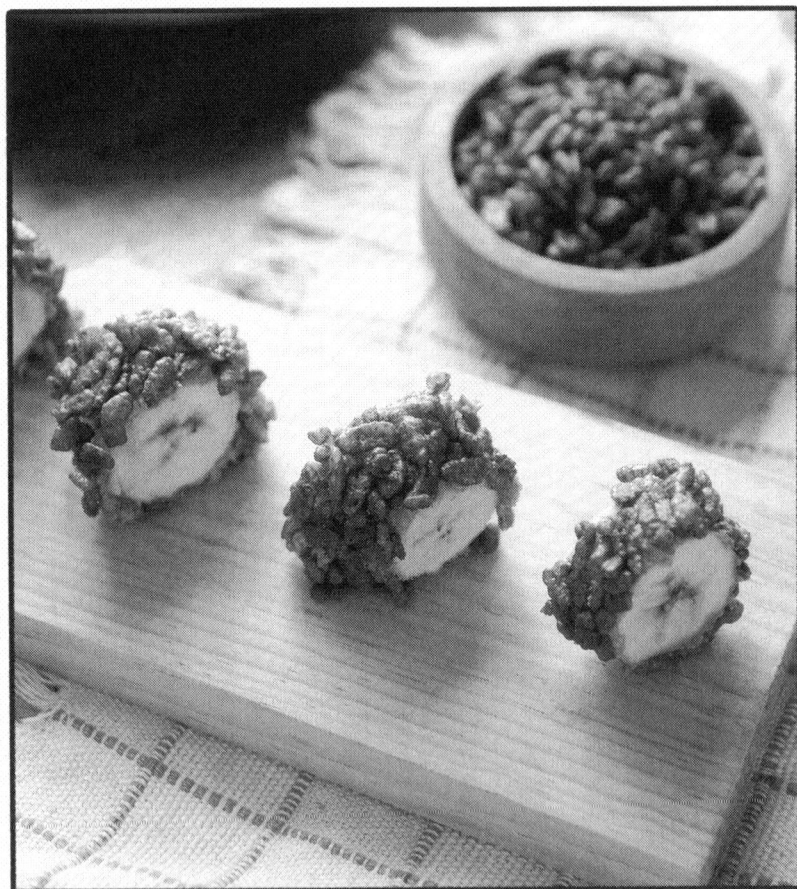

BANANA SUSHI

A FUN INTRODUCTION TO THE IDEA OF SUSHI IN A KID-FRIENDLY WAY! TRY USING BRIGHTLY COLORED CEREALS AS WELL AS A CHOCOLATE SYRUP DRIZZLE ON TOP FOR A FUN AND DELICIOUS LOOK.

INGREDIENTS

- BANANAS
- ALMOND BUTTER
- WHIPPED CREAM CHEESE
- COLORFUL CEREAL
- RICE CRISPY CEREAL
- SHREDDED COCONUT
- CHOCOLATE SYRUP
- CINNAMON SUGAR

DIRECTIONS

1. ROLL EACH BANANA IN ALMOND BUTTER OR WHIPPED CREAM CHEESE, AND ROLL IN ANY DESIRED COATING. DRIZZLE WITH CHOCOLATE SYRUP, OR SPRINKLE WITH CINNAMON SUGAR. FEEL FREE TO USE OTHER INGREDIENTS YOU HAVE ON HAND AS WELL!

2. CUT EACH BANANA INTO 6 PIECES AND EAT WITH CHOPSTICKS!

BROWNIE BATTER DIP

BROWNIE BATTER DIP

A DELICIOUS DESSERT DIP! WE RECOMMEND EATING WITH FRUIT, PRETZELS OR SHORTBREAD COOKIES.

INGREDIENTS

- 1 PACKAGE (8 OUNCES) CREAM CHEESE, SOFTENED
- 1/4 CUP BUTTER, SOFTENED
- 2 CUPS CONFECTIONERS' SUGAR
- 1/3 CUP BAKING COCOA
- 1/4 CUP MILK
- 2 TABLESPOONS BROWN SUGAR
- 1 TEASPOON VANILLA EXTRACT
- M&M'S MINIS, OPTIONAL
- ANIMAL CRACKERS, PRETZELS AND/OR SLICED APPLES

DIRECTIONS

IN A LARGE BOWL, BEAT CREAM CHEESE AND BUTTER UNTIL SMOOTH. BEAT IN CONFECTIONERS' SUGAR, COCOA, MILK, BROWN SUGAR AND VANILLA UNTIL SMOOTH. IF DESIRED, SPRINKLE WITH M&M'S MINIS. SERVE WITH DIPPERS OF YOUR CHOICE.

Recipes

BANANA PANCAKE SMOOTHIE

BANANA PANCAKE SMOOTHIE

THESE SMOOTHIES ARE A HEALTHY AND FUN TAKE ON BANANA PANCAKES. THEY ARE SURE TO BE A CROWD-PLEASER!

INGREDIENTS

- 1 CUP UNSWEETENED ALMOND MILK
- 1 MEDIUM BANANA
- 1/2 CUP FROZEN UNSWEETENED BLUEBERRIES
- 1/4 CUP INSTANT PLAIN OATMEAL
- 1 TEASPOON MAPLE SYRUP
- 1/2 TEASPOON GROUND CINNAMON
- DASH SEA SALT

DIRECTIONS

PLACE THE FIRST 6 INGREDIENTS IN A BLENDER; COVER AND PROCESS UNTIL SMOOTH. POUR INTO 2 CHILLED GLASSES; SPRINKLE WITH SEA SALT. SERVE IMMEDIATELY.

Recipes

CUCUMBER FACE MASK

Recipes

CUCUMBER FACE MASK

HOMEMADE CUCUMBER FACE MASKS ARE SAFE, NATURAL AND FUN!
PAMPER YOURSELF WHILE HYDRATING AND NOURISHING YOUR SKIN!

INGREDIENTS

- ONE CUCUMBER
- HALF A CUP OF PLAIN YOGURT
- A HANDFUL OF MINT LEAVES

DIRECTIONS

1. MIX CHOPPED CUCUMBER, YOGURT AND MINT IN BLENDER TO A THICK CONSISTENCY.

2. APPLY THE MIX ON THE SKIN AND LEAVE IT ON UNTIL IT DRIES.

3. REMOVE WITH WARM WATER FOR A REFRESHING EFFECT.

Recipes

BROWN SUGAR SCRUB EXFOLIATOR

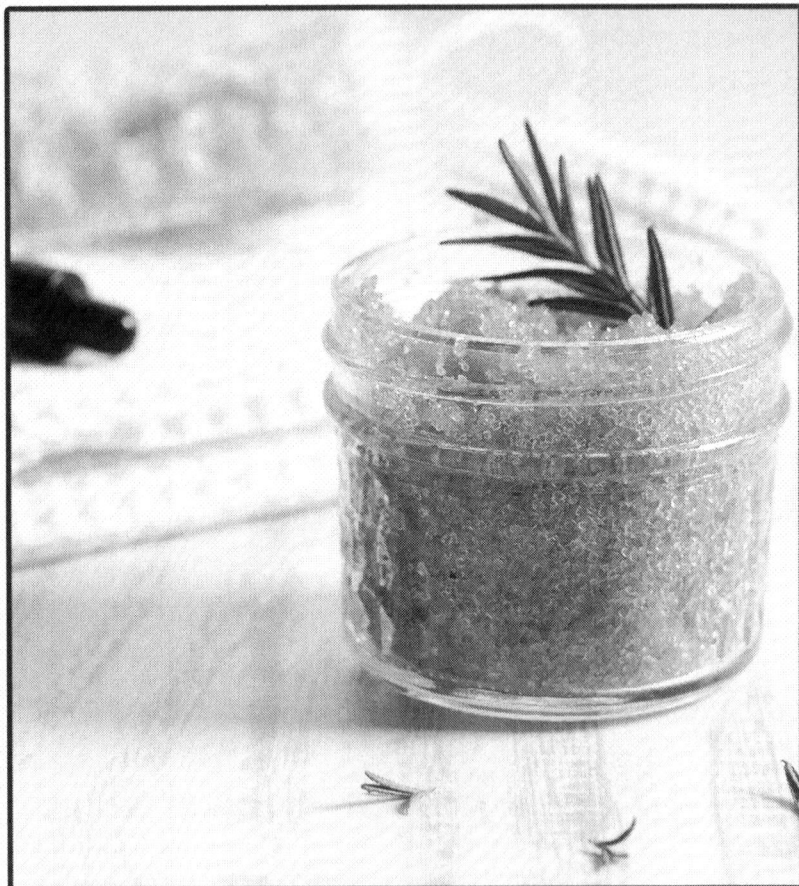

Recipes

BROWN SUGAR SCRUB EXFOLIATOR

THIS IS A FUN TAKE HOME GIFT FOR PARTY-GOERS, OR A FUN ACTIVITY TO DO DURING A SLUMBER PARTY. PLUS, IT SMELLS DELICIOUS!

INGREDIENTS

- 2 CUPS BROWN SUGAR
- 1 CUP SOLID (BUT SOFT) COCONUT OIL
- VANILLA EXTRACT

DIRECTIONS

1. WHIP TOGETHER THE SUGAR, OIL AND VANILLA UNTIL THE MIXTURE LOOKS CREAMY AND RESEMBLES LOOSE COOKIE DOUGH.

2. STORE IN AN AIRTIGHT CONTAINER.

3. OPEN AND STIR IT AROUND WITH YOUR FINGER BEFORE USING.

sleepover GAMES!

Party games!

TWO TRUTHS AND A LIE

Step 1

THE PLAYER NOMINATED TO GO FIRST SHARES THREE 'FACTS' ABOUT THEMSELF — TWO OF WHICH ARE TRUE, AND ONE WHICH IS NOT. FOR EXAMPLE, "I'VE BEEN TO THE GRAND CANYON, MY FAVORITE ICE CREAM IS MINT & CHIP, I HAVE TWO CATS."

Step 2

THE OTHER PLAYERS TRY TO GUESS WHICH TWO ARE TRUE AND WHICH IS THE LIE.

Step 3

THE PLAYERS WHO GUESS CORRECTLY ARE ALLOCATED ONE POINT.

Step 4

ONCE EVERY PLAYER HAS HAD A TURN AT SHARING THEIR 'FACTS,' THE PLAYER WHO HAS ACCUMULATED THE MOST POINTS WINS.

Party games!

HOT POLISH

Step 1

SIT THE GUESTS IN A CIRCLE.

Step 2

HAVE A FEW BOTTLES OF BRIGHTLY COLORED NAIL POLISH (HOW MANY WILL DEPEND ON THE SIZE OF YOUR GROUP), AND TURN ON THE TUNES.

Step 3

PLAYERS PASS THE BOTTLES QUICKLY AROUND THE CIRCLE CLOCKWISE, UNTIL THE MUSIC STOPS.

Step 4

PLAYERS HOLDING A BOTTLE WHEN THE MUSIC STOPS HAVE TO PAINT ONE OF THEIR TOENAILS THE COLOR THAT THEY'RE HOLDING.

Step 5

THEN THE MUSIC STARTS AGAIN AND PLAY REPEATS UNTIL EVERYONE'S TOENAILS ARE PAINTED.

Party games!

SLEEPING BEAUTY

Step 1

ONE PLAYER LAYS ON THEIR SLEEPING BAG OR BED AND PRETENDS TO BE ASLEEP.

Step 2

THE OTHER PLAYERS TAKE TURNS TRYING TO MAKE THE "SLEEPING" PLAYER LAUGH WITHOUT TOUCHING THEM.

Step 3

THE PLAYER THAT MAKES THE "SLEEPING" PLAYER LAUGH FIRST WINS THE GAME.

Party games!

FLASHLIGHT TAG

Step 1

HAVE EACH PERSON GET THEIR OWN FLASHLIGHT.

Step 2

FIND A SAFE AND DARK OUTDOOR PLACE LIKE A BACKYARD.

Step 3

ALL THE PLAYERS RACE TO FIND THEIR FRIENDS WITHOUT BEING DISCOVERED. WHEN A PLAYER FINDS SOMEONE, THEY SHINE THEIR LIGHT ON THEM AS THE WAY TO "TAG" THEM AND "FREEZE" THEM IN THEIR SPOT.

Step 4

THE LAST PERSON TO BE "FROZEN" WINS!

Party games!

SARDINES

Step 1

ONE PERSON HIDES. THE REST OF THE PARTY-GOERS BECOME SEEKERS.

Step 2

WHEN A SEEKER FINDS THE HIDDEN PERSON, THEY QUIETLY HIDE WITH THEM. PLAY CONTINUES WITH ALL PLAYERS CRAMMING INTO ONE SPACE UNTIL THERE IS ONLY ONE SEEKER LEFT.

Step 3

YOU'LL BE SURE TO DISCOVER JUST HOW MANY PEOPLE CAN SQUEEZE INTO ONE SPACE AND WHY IT'S CALLED SARDINES! THE LAST SEEKER LEFT BECOMES THE NEXT TO HIDE.

Party games!

FASHION SHOW

Step 1

GATHER ALUMINUM FOIL, TOILET PAPER, RIBBONS AND FABRIC SCRAPS.

Step 2

SPLIT SLUMBER PARTY ATTENDEES INTO TWO TEAMS.

Step 3

GIVE THE TEAMS A SET TIME LIMIT TO CREATE A ONE-OF-A-KIND DRESS ON A SELECTED TEAM MEMBER. GET CREATIVE!

Step 4

FASHION SHOW TIME! HAVE THE ELEGANTLY OUTFITTED PLAYERS SHOW OFF THEIR NEW CREATIONS BY WALKING DOWN THE AISLE LIKE SUPERMODELS.

Party games!

NEON DANCE PARTY

Step 1

BUY SOME GLOW-IN-THE-DARK NECKLACES, BRACELETS AND OTHER ACCESSORIES.

Step 2

MAKE A PLAYLIST OF EVERYONE'S FAVORITE SONGS.

Step 3

TURN OFF THE LIGHTS, AND ENJOY THE DANCE PARTY!

Party games!

TELEPHONE

Step 1

PLAYERS SIT IN A CIRCLE OR STAND IN A LINE - CLOSE ENOUGH THAT WHISPERING IS POSSIBLE, BUT NOT SO CLOSE THAT PLAYERS CAN HEAR EACH OTHER WHISPER.

Step 2

THE FIRST PERSON IN THE CIRCLE WHISPERS A SENTENCE INTO THE EAR OF THE PERSON SITTING OR STANDING TO THEIR RIGHT. THE SILLIER THE BETTER!

Step 3

THAT PERSON THEN WHISPERS THE PHRASE INTO THE EAR OF THE PERSON ON THEIR RIGHT. CONTINUE THAT WAY UNTIL IT REACHES THE LAST PLAYER.

Step 4

THE LAST PLAYER SAYS THE SENTENCE OR PHRASE OUT LOUD SO EVERYONE CAN HEAR HOW MUCH IT HAS CHANGED FROM THE FIRST WHISPER AT THE BEGINNING OF THE CIRCLE OR LINE!

Party games!

TOSS AND TALK BALL

Step 1

BLOW UP AN INFLATABLE BEACH BALL.

Step 2

WRITE A BUNCH OF INTERESTING QUESTIONS ALL OVER IT USING A PERMANENT MARKER.

Step 3

THE KIDS CAN SIT ON THEIR SLEEPING BAGS THEN TOSS THE BALL TO ONE ANOTHER.

Step 4

THE CATCHER MUST ANSWER THE QUESTION CLOSEST TO THEIR RIGHT INDEX FINGER BEFORE SENDING THE BALL ONTO THE NEXT PLAYER.

Party games!

RIGHT, LEFT, EAT

Step 1

GIVE EVERYONE THREE PIECES OF CANDY AND HAVE THEM SIT IN A LARGE CIRCLE EITHER ON THE GROUND OR AT A TABLE.

Step 2

STARTING WITH THE SLUMBER PARTY HOST, PLAYERS ROLL AS MANY DICE AS THEY HAVE PIECES OF CANDY, UP TO THREE. ON THEIR FIRST ROLL WITH THREE PIECES OF CANDY, THEY WOULD ROLL THREE DICE. IF THEY HAVE ONE PIECE OF CANDY LEFT, THEY WOULD ROLL ONE DIE.

Step 3

AFTER ROLLING THE DICE: IF A '1' IS ROLLED, THEY WOULD PASS ONE CANDY TO THE RIGHT. IF A '2' IS ROLLED, THEY WOULD PASS ONE CANDY TO THE LEFT. IF A '3' IS ROLLED, THEY WOULD EAT THE CANDY. AND IF A '4', '5', OR '6' IS ROLLED, THEY WOULD KEEP THE CANDY. SO IF THE PLAYER ROLLS ONE '1', ONE '2', AND ONE '6', THEY WOULD PASS ONE CANDY LEFT, ONE CANDY RIGHT, AND KEEP ONE CANDY. WHEN THAT PLAYER'S TURN IS OVER, THE PERSON TO THE RIGHT OF THEM TAKES THEIR TURN.

Step 4

CONTINUE PASSING THE DICE AROUND THE CIRCLE LETTING PEOPLE ROLL, PASSING OR EATING THE CANDY, UNTIL ONLY ONE PERSON IS LEFT WITH CANDY. THAT PERSON WINS THE GAME AND A SMALL PRIZE.

M.A.S.H.

89

M.A.S.H.

INSTRUCTIONS

....

1. M.A.S.H. IS A FUN GAME THAT PREDICTS YOUR FUTURE LIFE. M.A.S.H. STANDS FOR MANSION, APARTMENT, SHACK OR HOUSE.

2. TO START, FILL IN FOUR OPTIONS FOR EACH CATEGORY (OPTIONAL – HAVE YOUR FRIEND CHOOSE THE LAST OPTION FOR EACH CATEGORY).

3. CLOSE YOUR EYES AND LET YOUR FRIEND MAKE SMALL LINES IN THE MIDDLE OF THE PAPER UNTIL YOU SAY, "STOP." COUNT THOSE LINES, AND WRITE IT INSIDE THE HEART IN THE MIDDLE OF THE PAGE.

   IF PLAYING ALONE, CLOSE YOUR EYES AND QUICKLY DRAW A SPIRAL IN THE MIDDLE OF THE PAGE. AFTER 5-10 SECONDS, STOP, OPEN YOUR EYES, AND COUNT HOW MANY RINGS ARE IN THE SPIRAL. THEN, WRITE THIS NUMBER IN THE HEART.

4. USING YOUR NUMBER, COUNT OUT THAT MANY OF YOUR OPTIONS, STARTING WITH M.A.S.H. THEN, STRIKE OUT THE OPTION YOUR NUMBER LANDS ON, AND REPEAT.

5. WHEN ALL BUT ONE OPTION IN A CATEGORY IS STRUCK OUT, CIRCLE THE REMAINING ONE.

6. WHEN EVERY CATEGORY IS FINISHED, READ YOUR FULL FORTUNE OUT LOUD.

M.A.S.H.

MANSION   APARTMENT   SHACK   HOUSE

FUTURE SPOUSE

1.
2.
3.
4.

NUMBER OF KIDS

1.
2.
3.
4.

FUTURE CAR

1.
2.
3.
4.

FUTURE JOB

1.
2.
3.
4.

WRITE YOUR
NUMBER HERE:

FIRST CHILD'S NAME

1.
2.
3.
4.

SPOUSE'S JOB

1.
2.
3.
4.

FUTURE PET

1.
2.
3.
4.

CITY YOU LIVE IN

1.
2.
3.
4.

M.A.S.H.

MANSION   APARTMENT   SHACK   HOUSE

FUTURE SPOUSE
1.
2.
3.
4.

NUMBER OF KIDS
1.
2.
3.
4.

FUTURE CAR
1.
2.
3.
4.

FUTURE JOB
1.
2.
3.
4.

WRITE YOUR NUMBER HERE:

FIRST CHILD'S NAME
1.
2.
3.
4.

SPOUSE'S JOB
1.
2.
3.
4.

FUTURE PET
1.
2.
3.
4.

CITY YOU LIVE IN
1.
2.
3.
4.

M.A.S.H.

MANSION   APARTMENT   SHACK   HOUSE

FUTURE SPOUSE
1.
2.
3.
4.

NUMBER OF KIDS
1.
2.
3.
4.

FUTURE CAR
1.
2.
3.
4.

FUTURE JOB
1.
2.
3.
4.

WRITE YOUR
NUMBER HERE:

FIRST CHILD'S NAME
1.
2.
3.
4.

SPOUSE'S JOB
1.
2.
3.
4.

FUTURE PET
1.
2.
3.
4.

CITY YOU LIVE IN
1.
2.
3.
4.

M.A.S.H.

MANSION   APARTMENT   SHACK   HOUSE

FUTURE SPOUSE
1.
2.
3.
4.

NUMBER OF KIDS
1.
2.
3.
4.

FUTURE CAR
1.
2.
3.
4.

FUTURE JOB
1.
2.
3.
4.

WRITE YOUR
NUMBER HERE:

FIRST CHILD'S NAME
1.
2.
3.
4.

SPOUSE'S JOB
1.
2.
3.
4.

FUTURE PET
1.
2.
3.
4.

CITY YOU LIVE IN
1.
2.
3.
4.

M.A.S.H.

MANSION   APARTMENT   SHACK   HOUSE

FUTURE SPOUSE
1.
2.
3.
4.

NUMBER OF KIDS
1.
2.
3.
4.

FUTURE CAR
1.
2.
3.
4.

FUTURE JOB
1.
2.
3.
4.

WRITE YOUR
NUMBER HERE:

FIRST CHILD'S NAME
1.
2.
3.
4.

SPOUSE'S JOB
1.
2.
3.
4.

FUTURE PET
1.
2.
3.
4.

CITY YOU LIVE IN
1.
2.
3.
4.

M.A.S.H.

MANSION   APARTMENT   SHACK   HOUSE

FUTURE SPOUSE
1.
2.
3.
4.

NUMBER OF KIDS
1.
2.
3.
4.

FUTURE CAR
1.
2.
3.
4.

FUTURE JOB
1.
2.
3.
4.

WRITE YOUR NUMBER HERE:

FIRST CHILD'S NAME
1.
2.
3.
4.

SPOUSE'S JOB
1.
2.
3.
4.

FUTURE PET
1.
2.
3.
4.

CITY YOU LIVE IN
1.
2.
3.
4.

M.A.S.H.

MANSION   APARTMENT   SHACK   HOUSE

FUTURE SPOUSE	NUMBER OF KIDS	FUTURE CAR
1.	1.	1.
2.	2.	2.
3.	3.	3.
4.	4.	4.

FUTURE JOB		FIRST CHILD'S NAME
1.		1.
2.		2.
3.		3.
4.	WRITE YOUR NUMBER HERE: ♥	4.

SPOUSE'S JOB	FUTURE PET	CITY YOU LIVE IN
1.	1.	1.
2.	2.	2.
3.	3.	3.
4.	4.	4.

M.A.S.H.

MANSION APARTMENT SHACK HOUSE

FUTURE SPOUSE
1.
2.
3.
4.

NUMBER OF KIDS
1.
2.
3.
4.

FUTURE CAR
1.
2.
3.
4.

FUTURE JOB
1.
2.
3.
4.

WRITE YOUR
NUMBER HERE:

FIRST CHILD'S NAME
1.
2.
3.
4.

SPOUSE'S JOB
1.
2.
3.
4.

FUTURE PET
1.
2.
3.
4.

CITY YOU LIVE IN
1.
2.
3.
4.

M.A.S.H.

MANSION   APARTMENT   SHACK   HOUSE

FUTURE SPOUSE	NUMBER OF KIDS	FUTURE CAR
1.	1.	1.
2.	2.	2.
3.	3.	3.
4.	4.	4.

FUTURE JOB		FIRST CHILD'S NAME
1.		1.
2.		2.
3.		3.
4.	WRITE YOUR NUMBER HERE: ♥	4.

SPOUSE'S JOB	FUTURE PET	CITY YOU LIVE IN
1.	1.	1.
2.	2.	2.
3.	3.	3.
4.	4.	4.

M.A.S.H.

MANSION   APARTMENT   SHACK   HOUSE

FUTURE SPOUSE
1.
2.
3.
4.

NUMBER OF KIDS
1.
2.
3.
4.

FUTURE CAR
1.
2.
3.
4.

FUTURE JOB
1.
2.
3.
4.

WRITE YOUR NUMBER HERE:

FIRST CHILD'S NAME
1.
2.
3.
4.

SPOUSE'S JOB
1.
2.
3.
4.

FUTURE PET
1.
2.
3.
4.

CITY YOU LIVE IN
1.
2.
3.
4.

M.A.S.H.

MANSION   APARTMENT   SHACK   HOUSE

FUTURE SPOUSE
1.
2.
3.
4.

NUMBER OF KIDS
1.
2.
3.
4.

FUTURE CAR
1.
2.
3.
4.

FUTURE JOB
1.
2.
3.
4.

WRITE YOUR NUMBER HERE:

FIRST CHILD'S NAME
1.
2.
3.
4.

SPOUSE'S JOB
1.
2.
3.
4.

FUTURE PET
1.
2.
3.
4.

CITY YOU LIVE IN
1.
2.
3.
4.

all DONE!

IF YOU LOVED THIS SLUMBER PARTY BOOK, THEN YOU WILL LOVE THE REST OF THE QUIZ BOSS SERIES OF BOOKS, LIKE:

⭐ WOULD YOU RATHER AND MORE! - GIRLS EDITION

⭐ WOULD YOU RATHER AND MORE! - BOYS EDITION

⭐ ALL ABOUT ME JOURNAL

⭐ THE ULTIMATE SUMMER VACATION BOOK

FIND ALL OF OUR BOOKS ON AMAZON,
AND DON'T FORGET TO LEAVE US A REVIEW!

WWW.QUIZBOSS.CO

Printed in Great Britain
by Amazon

50912487R00057